CHARLES RENNIE MACKINTOSH

PHOTOGRAPHS BY
COLIN BAXTER

TEXT BY
JOHN McKEAN

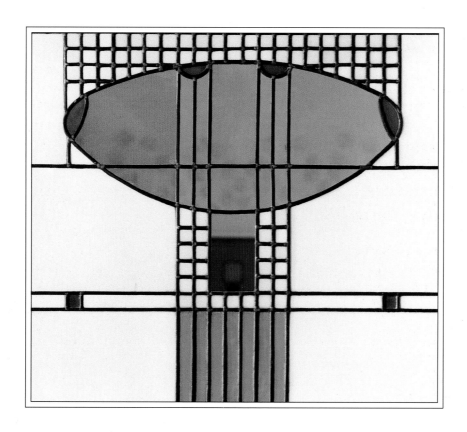

Colin Baxter Photography, Grantown-on-Spey, Scotland

CHARLES RENNIE MACKINTOSH

Glasgow, just over a century ago. The booming 'second city' of the British Empire, made rich on a century of commercial capital in cotton and tobacco, now become the centre of heavy engineering production. Ships and engines, requiring technologists and fitters and designers from technical college and from art school. Acres of four-storey walls filled with tiny dwellings for the exploited labour and, in other parts, with spacious suburban flats stuffed with the clutter of the bourgeoisie. The grandiose civic bombast of department store, bank headquarters, warehouse and hotel. Typically, on the corner of Charing Cross, on Sauchiehall Street in the city centre, an ornate French-wedding-cake block of shops and flats built in 1891 to the designs of architect J. J. Burnet.

The Artist at 25

One weekend a couple of years after Charing Cross Mansions was built (and unaware, as he looks up at it, that Burnet would one day be his client at the School of Art), 25-year-old Charles Rennie Mackintosh enters the Sauchiehall Street studio of his friend, the photographer J. Craig Annan. He is to sit for his portrait. He had put on a pale tweed jacket and a loose-collared white shirt. A wonderfully long, green Liberty scarf is loosely knotted in a large bow – in what's known as *style libre* – as a tie round his neck. That day, Annan and Mackintosh produce a series of portraits. He looks out of the picture into the future, moustache perfectly curled, slightly droopy left eye, and tiny kiss-curl on his forehead. Who is this man?

For ten years already (from his mid teens), each weekday from early till late, young Mr Mackintosh has been working in architects' offices. Late-Victorian architects were sober men – all men without a doubt – concerned with their

MACKINTOSH AGED 25 is photographed by Annan in 1893 not as assistant architect but as interior artist. Against a background of dark, late-Victorian design, Mackintosh's own room, opposite (1900, recreated 1906) is all Art: pureness of space, simplicity of form, sparing elegance of line, subtle pale colour.

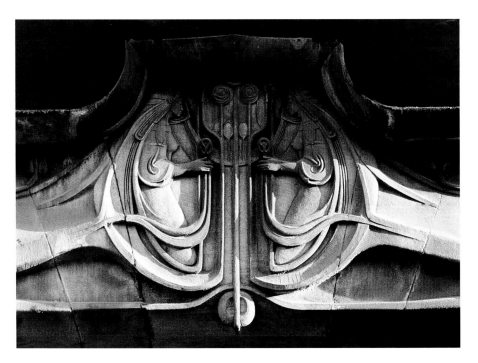

THE SYMBOLIC ARTIST permeates his architecture: muses flanking a rosebush ornament the keystone over his new School of Art entrance (1897-8), above; his famous abstracted rose graphic, here stencilled on the bedroom wardrobe at Windyhill (1901), below.

standing in society as professionals; they wore high, starched collars and dark, three-piece suits. A fob-watch helped complete the picture. On this day, Mr Mackintosh is defining a new image for himself, as a dandy. His father, a strict Presbyterian Highlander in the Glasgow police force, had even been against his 16-year-old son's wish to become a respectable professional architect. But now the young man – known to friends as 'Toshie', who signed himself Chas R. Mackintosh (and certainly would not be called 'Rennie Mackintosh') – is transforming himself further: from architect to designer and artist.

This double life, of architect and artist, had its first hint when, even before he started in an architectural job, Mackintosh enrolled in the School of Art for evening classes. So from his teens, the practical, masculine and dour world of construction and the bright, romantic and feminine world of art began to form dual paths. Through the 1890s, from the time of this portrait session, these strands, easily polarised as black and white, seem to run alongside each other, almost as a dangerous double life, until Mackintosh can finally integrate his different talents into a few great works in the years after the turn of the century. Between 1900 and 1905, in his early thirties, he will draw together these different strands, in his life and in his art. ('Life' is the leaves which shape and nourish a plant, he says, but 'art' is the flower which embodies its meaning.)

In those few years, he will be able not only to create magical interior spaces, ordered and formed, decorated and furnished with exquisite surfaces and objects, but also, to create places formed within a skin of his own designing, within an architectural form and organisation. But that unity will not last.

Mackintosh's first mystical, symbolist watercolour. A naked female form floats below the melancholic angel of The Harvest Moon *(1892).*

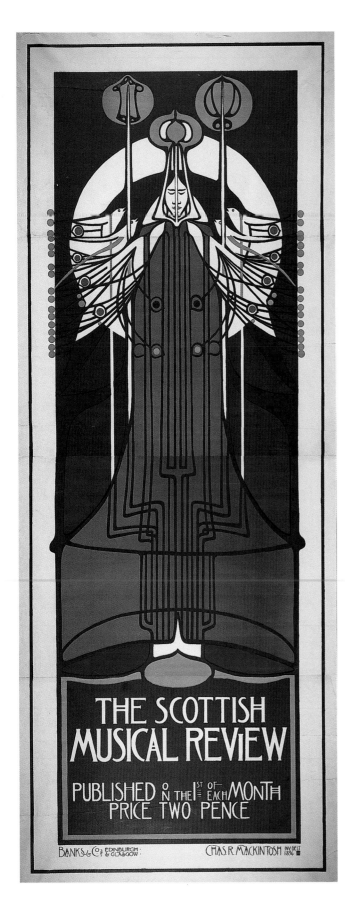

Though his talents are irrepressible, the influence behind his work after 1905 – the vagaries of fashion and of patronage, and indeed the vagaries of his own depressive temperament and shaky self-confidence – will never allow his unique abilities to all work together in such a way again. Within another decade, his career will retreat to the two-dimensional, to flower-studies, textile and graphic design, and eventually end with a wonderful series of watercolour landscape paintings as far from architecture and interior spaces as were his early symbolic watercolours or youthful posters and lettering.

But it was an architect he set out to be. Like his great predecessor Alexander ('Greek') Thomson 50 years earlier, Mackintosh is a first-generation Glaswegian without the advantage of an urban, educated background. While there may have been virtually no books beyond the Bible in either home when these lads started on their architectural apprenticeship, at least Mackintosh had schooling. He spent five years at Allan Glen's, well-known for offering a sound technical education to the children of artisans, before starting his apprenticeship with an unknown Glasgow architect at the age of 16.

With that pupilage over, when he was 21 he was freed to join the leading late-Victorian architect John Honeyman as draughtsman. This is the office where his whole architectural career is contained. John Keppie, a young architect there and soon to become Honeyman's partner, now befriends the younger Mackintosh. Visits to the Keppies become frequent, but before long they are as much to court his colleague's sister, Jessie, as to meet with John. At the same time another draughtsman at Honeyman's, Herbert McNair, moustachioed and dressed so similarly they might be twins, becomes Toshie's closest friend.

When Mackintosh wins a travelling scholarship, letting him break from the office, his first plan is to spend nine months abroad. The scholarship couldn't cover that, and he slowly toured north through Italy on his own from March 1891, returning with increased confidence in July. As the 1890s open up, Mackintosh and McNair, through Jessie Keppie, who is a full-time day student at the School of Art, and to whom Mackintosh is now formally engaged in 1892, both enter a quite new, largely feminine, circle of young artists and designers. The contrast of the all-male architectural daytime reality and the art school evening imagination is sharpened. They form a group who dub themselves 'The Immortals', spending evenings and weekends wrapped in symbolic and allegorical image-making. Mackintosh designs his first furniture (for a painter friend; some is today in the Hunterian Museum) and joins The Immortals in decorative arts, graphics projects and symbolic paintings which they publish themselves in 1893 and 1894, alongside their own writing, in various issues of what they call *The Magazine*.

Meanwhile, the other life at Honeyman's has produced a nondescript pair of houses for Mackintosh relatives (140-2 Balgrayhill Road), interior work at Craigie

ARCHITECT BY DAY creates Queen's Cross Church, above (1897). Artist by night publishes a watercolour, 'Autumn', in The Magazine *(1894) and derives this 8 ft (2.5 m) tall poster, opposite, from its design.*

Hall and the Glasgow Art Club (which are claimed by Keppie) and the large *Glasgow Herald* warehouse (today The Lighthouse) in Mitchell Street.

In 1894, as Keppie's assistant, he works on Queen Margaret College (today altered beyond recognition); in 1895 he is in charge of Martyrs' School (which still exists); and in 1896 he produces one of the office schemes to be entered in competition for much-needed new, purpose-built premises for the art school where, for many years up to 1895, he had himself enrolled as a student.

MARGARET MACDONALD'S exquisite gesso panel, above, hangs over the studio fireplace in the house she and CRM created together. MMM in a Mackintosh chair, below.

Artistic Life and the Artistic Interior

The work of The Immortal artists, meanwhile, matures and becomes more individual. Two of the strongest members, sisters Frances and Margaret Macdonald, with a chance to exhibit their work, find it called 'clever', 'weird' and 'hideous' by the local press. The term 'spook school' begins to encompass Mackintosh alongside them. Now moving ever closer to these sisters personally as well as artistically, Mackintosh breaks his engagement to Jessie Keppie. He designs a poster whose not-too-veiled eroticism is based on Beardsley; he designs wall stencils for a Glasgow tea room; and with the Macdonald sisters he exhibits work at the Arts and Crafts Society in London. While mostly ignored by critics, this show results in an article on them in *The Studio*, a journal fashionably read around Europe; Mackintosh's first press coverage illustrates a mural and some furniture.

But by now, in 1897, Mackintosh's intimate relationship with Margaret Macdonald, alongside his friend McNair's with her sister Frances, sees them rising beyond the student Immortals, to become known as 'The Four'. Squeezed ever closer together in the great crescendo from 1895 to 1900, they work together (and sometimes jointly, with Toshie always the most independent) across the decorative arts. (The other three publish work alongside Oscar Wilde in *The Yellow Book*.) Mackintosh is commissioned for a bedroom, which becomes his first white interior with integrated furniture. An article in Germany on the group's work is followed by commissions to Mackintosh, with Margaret's beaten metal panels on the furniture, for a dining room built for that magazine's editor in Munich,

and then a first white living room, built for Margaret's parents. The climax for The Four is an 1899 invitation to show decorative and interior work in London; during the exhibition, Frances Macdonald and Herbert McNair are married.

Early in 1900, Mackintosh designs his first tea room interior (Ingram Street Ladies' Luncheon Room, recreated for the 1996 travelling exhibition), dominated by a pair of vast and wonderfully romantic gesso panels on facing walls, designed and made by Margaret and himself. At the same time, they together put their hearts into the complete make-over of a flat on the corner of Blythswood Square, where they would live, after their own wedding in August. This would epitomise both their fusion and the fusion of life with art; pure, refined, white and subtly coloured, framing exquisite objects, sensual surfaces and jewel-like use of materials.

MACKINTOSH (CRM) AND MACDONALD (MMM) mingle. Another CRM rose inlaid in a 1901 bookcase, above; two MMM leaded glass roundels (1900) which hang in their own drawing room, below.

The interiors of the late '90s are finally celebrated by an invitation to these artists from the famously avant-garde Secession in Vienna. The Four, preparing this exhibition in 1900, are all together one last time (the McNairs had moved to Liverpool in '99). The

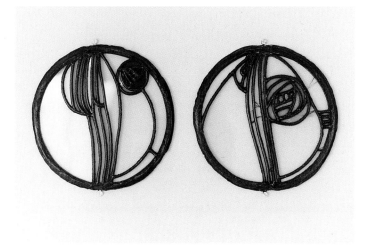

Mackintoshes travel to install it, incorporating much of the furnishings from their own new flat. They are fêted; it seems a second honeymoon, if a rather odd one, with much of their own wedding furniture on exhibit. One Vienna paper talks of 'the most striking interiors modern art has created' but others, like the 'spook school' headlines at their first public showing, talk of 'hobgoblins' and 'torture chambers'. Five years earlier, Margaret had been encouraging Toshie to climb up alongside her; but now he must move on ahead. Leaving the McNairs and so many other formulaic 'Glasgow style' designers behind, for the time being he still takes Margaret by the hand.

HIS MASTERPIECE, the Glasgow School of Art, is opened, half-built, in 1899. The gallery, with its barn-like wooden trusses softened by little hearts, above. Opposite: the north front, with its dynamic symmetry, is completed exactly a decade later. A typical clock face, below.

The School of Art

Back with life at Honeyman & Keppie: architecture is tough, big, bold and based on simple basic ideas; it is dark, serious, masculine. With Honeyman now retired, Mackintosh's relationship with Keppie is barely civil: unforgiving of the jilting of his sister Jessie, John Keppie seems equally unforgiving of his young colleague's obviously superior ease and facility in designing and drawing, and his spreading fame beyond their architectural business. But it is also here, back in Keppie's office, that Mackintosh's real break has come. In January 1897 his entry wins the School of Art competition. The governors, however, only have money for half; building starts, but not until years later will they decide to complete the project. By that time Mackintosh will have a quite different maturity; more fully in control, he will completely revise a new western end, to be finished exactly a decade after the first half, in December 1909. So this building, his masterpiece, is virtually his first and will be virtually his last building as

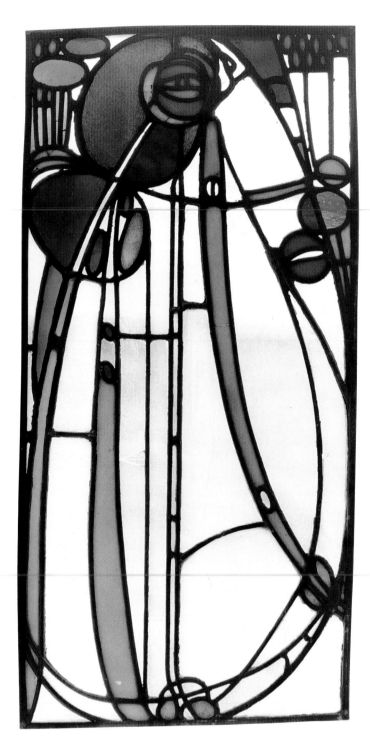

AMIDST CHAIRS AND LIGHTS from their own home, the Mackintoshes also design new elements for The Rose Boudoir exhibition in Italy (1902), including this leaded glass panel.

architect. Mackintosh's architectural work is that of a man in his thirties.

While the School of Art is being detailed, and constructed (with John Keppie running the job on site and preparing to take credit for its design also), Mackintosh designs his only church (Queen's Cross Church, 1897).

The School of Art opens as an odd, half-building in the last days of 1899. If Mackintosh is not credited widely with the design, there's no press coverage anyway. It's nearly a century before Robert Venturi will call its street façade one of the greatest achievements of all time, comparable in scale and majesty to Michelangelo. From the director's suite above the castle-like entrance to the great studios or the double bay-windowed boardroom, the building is a series of linked interior experiences, strung along a promenade from the tiny low door at the top of its tall steps, to the forest-like stairwell and roof-lit hall above, from which other rooms lead. It brilliantly integrates overall architectural form and interior place-making, right down to the tiniest detail of door-handle, leaded-glass insert or name-plate. This range of concerns is balanced without any 'Modernist' worry about making them speak the same language.

This building leads to Mackintosh's most integrated years. Paradoxically, the little fame he attracts – and that is entirely outside Britain – still rests on developments from before the turn of the century: not on his architecture in the office, only on his private reputation in decorative arts and individual room-settings.

So he accepts interiors: local domestic interiors, a music room in Vienna and then an important exhibition for Turin in 1902 as well as a room-setting for Moscow. The head of the School of Art, Fra Newbery, by now Mackintosh's good friend, organises the Turin show; Toshie is architect and, with Margaret, he creates the exquisite room setting The Rose Boudoir (elements of which remain in their own reconstructed house today). The Willow's five different tea room spaces are fitted out in 1903, as well as a bedroom setting for exhibition in Dresden. Then, in one 1904 project Mackintosh creates half-a-

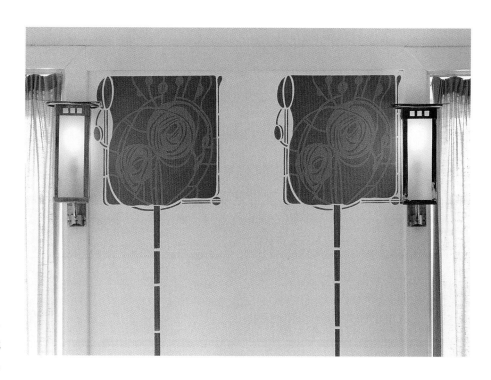

dozen complete room settings, and even more furniture than for his recently finished Hill House. This is at the early nineteenth-century country house Hous'hill (by then in suburban Glasgow) whose name, originally 'Howsle', means 'a pretty dwelling and a reasonably good house'. Here, for Miss Catherine Cranston, patron of his tea rooms, he ensures it lives up to that name, with a completely re-formed interior.

WITH HIS FIRST HOUSE, WINDYHILL (1899-1901), we see the contrasting CRM worlds: the bedroom interior, above, is modern, artistic, delicate. The vernacular exterior, below, at first glance seems traditional. Yet it too is quite unlike the contemporary English brick. Here elemental geometric forms and window holes suggest a new use of a more local tradition.

From 1900, his interiors are not just fashionable *fin-de-siècle* décor as produced around Glasgow by various of his contemporaries; nor are they like the pragmatic, anti-symbolic work of his English contemporary, C.A. Voysey. Each space, and the succession of spaces, is based on precisely controlled underlying geometry, and an inventive symbolism which is always more or less discernible.

So Mackintosh is supported by his brilliant design eye and facility in the minor arts – in graphics and in furniture, in design of cutlery, furnishing fabric or just the artistic arrangement of dried flowers. But now, into the new century, his confidence as architect and as interior place-maker are finally matched. He receives the personal commission of a detached house (Windyhill, still a private house today)

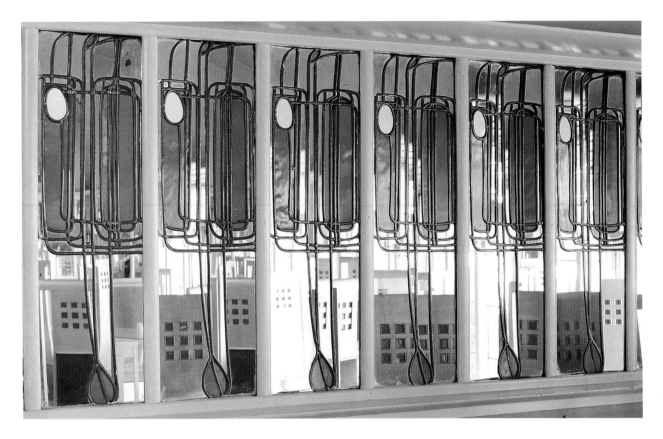

THE ROOM DE LUXE (1903) at CRM's last tea room, the Willow in Sauchiehall Street, is restored and back in business, above, while the House for an Art Lover project (1900-1), below, has, 90 years later and with great care and expense, become vast, country house reality.

in 1900; while that is being built, he enters an 'ideas competition' for a much larger house and, though it does not win that competition, his project is published as an exquisite portfolio of drawings (House for an Art Lover, now reconstructed in south Glasgow).

By 1902, having become a partner, and the firm now called Honeyman, Keppie & Mackintosh, he personally is commissioned for another, larger, suburban house (The Hill House, Helensburgh, his domestic masterpiece, now owned by The National Trust for Scotland). Just as its roof is completed a year later, he lands his most memorable Cranston Tea Room, The Willow (partly reconstructed today) which is quickly on site and completed, a few months before The Hill House, in late 1903. No wonder he needs an early summer holiday in Orkney following overwork! Yet, that same summer Mackintosh takes on the design of a large board school which has been offered to the office (Scotland Street School, today an education museum).

The Integrated Years

The architect and artist in Mackintosh seemed a few years earlier to be two, parallel lives. Finally they no longer occupy separate worlds; no longer parallel opposites of day and night, of darkness and brightness, masculinity and femininity, and so on.

Now, as the integrated personality is reflected in the flat which makes their own marriage concrete, so Mackintosh integrates his different talents into his great works in the years after the turn of the century. The years 1900-1905 are those of his key achievement in the successful fusion of interiors, furniture and architectural form. Now he confidently, explicitly, uses these polarities of light and dark in his own work; playing with them, holding the two extremes in dynamic equilibrium. At its most obvious, this is seen (say at The Hill House) in the journey from the dark, protective, heavy entrance towards the softest, light, white spaces at the building's heart. At one extreme is the hard shell, characterised by the adjectives strong, sober, empiricist, objective. This is essentially a variant on the vernacular, on tradition.

At the other end is the white interior, which attracts adjectives such as soft, decorated, idealist, fantastic, erotic; and this is essentially creative and modern. So the outside often shows one conservative extreme: clearly seen at the School of Art, the two country houses or Scotland Street School. The deepest interior

A SOARING STAIR-TOWER at Scotland Street School (1906) where traditional form mingles with daring new detail – exemplary precision of masonry and glass under its conical slated hat.

THE HILL HOUSE HALLWAY, above, with clock, chair and extraordinary lights leads up under dark joists to the pure, pale and refined master bedroom, opposite.

space, shows the other, progressive, extreme: as in the main bedroom at Windyhill or The Hill House, but also in the Director's room in the School of Art.

Other main rooms play variations along this spectrum, libraries tending to the dark (more traditional and more sober); drawing rooms tending to the light; a black corridor door illuminated by sparks of deep ruby glass opens to reveal that it is painted white on the reverse (in an art school studio or a master bedroom) where those glass spots now appear an opaque pink.

Linking the extremes, symbolically but also literally, are hallways and stairs. These intermediate spaces are not just fascinating but perhaps – in performing a mediating role between the masculine, rather dour, tradition-conscious public world, and the feminine, almost dreamlike, fantastic and freely creative private world – they are his most important creations. And he loves to play with them: how the tight, dark, vaulted School of Art entrance opens into the top-lit stairwell beyond; the little, ambiguous sitting spaces in corridors; the glazed 'hen-run' and scooped-out loggia at the top of the dark School of Art end stairs; a half-hidden landing at The Hill House; the hall and the fantastic stair cylinders at Scotland Street School...

Mackintosh's particular talent lies in the design and articulation of space and

*THE HILL HOUSE,
Helensburgh (1902-4),
CRM's domestic masterpiece.
The south front, above, shows
the traditional 'baronial'
image with harled wall
surface, steep slate roofs,
chimneys and pencil-shaped
stair tower. A closer look
shows a carefully composed
range of window shapes,
from the tiny one by the
main bed (far left) to the
children's fantastic look-out
(top right). The five-part
drawing room bay, seen from
inside (opposite), simply
sticks out as a cube.*

form, of material and shape in three dimensions, where the scale is intimate and the engineering constraints few. It is a middle ground between his work in graphics, textiles and the design of small objects on one hand, and that creation of a complex new plan arrangement and structural envelope – what we usually think of today as the centre of an architect's job – on the other.

He can play the world of the more transitory interior artist and shop fitter against that of the strong architectural exterior, a skin to be expressive in form and detail. On occasions he simply brings the skin to life and forgets the interior (as with his two newspaper warehouses); on others he had no control of the envelope at all (as in his own homes or almost all the tea room work). But where he could deal with both, he balances these domains as separate worlds of inside and out. Layering the interior spaces to make the rooms speak and, at the same time, articulating the exterior form for it appropriately to fit in, to speak to the town, be heard and understood in its context, these are separate tasks. The exterior world encloses and protects a quite different one inside.

How does Mackintosh build this up? First, his buildings always have a traditional base. This is not just in what they look like: Mackintosh's inspiration in old buildings and especially in the old castles and tower houses of Scotland, is a deep and unnostalgic inspiration. But the traditional base is also in their layout: in the standard school plan, the typical Edwardian middle-class house layout, or

in the straightforward common sense organisation of an art school.

Second, within an appropriate skin and on top of the traditional plan layout, Mackintosh shapes each form with the touch of a sure place-maker, a skill which is nothing to do with stylish fancy or fashion. He has no problem using the newest of materials, whether for hidden structure or decorative finish, but has no interest in an image of 'newness'. So he mixes structural materials in an adhoc way, the goal always being the intended surface and space. At the School of Art, overhanging ends of structural steels are split and hammered into curves more like a broken stick of celery.

Third, inside these places, whether in a new or an existing old shell, he further layers each with its own particularly formed smaller places, often like rooms within rooms; areas under their own lowered ceilings, or carved into the thickness of walls; or by grouping his tall-backed chairs to form spaces.

Finally, the last layer, the surfaces, speak equally eloquently – shiny polished wood against rough planking, extraordinary metal light fittings in luminous colours, tiny glass inserts in wall panels, subtle plaster curves; down to the decorative

IN THE DRAWING ROOM, with delicately stencilled walls (detail below), bays extend beyond the cubic room shape with its higher, pale ceiling.

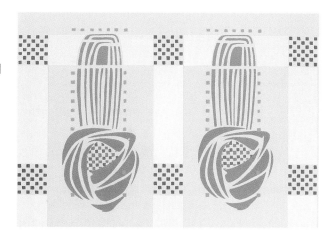

THEIR OWN CONVERTED terrace house (1906) contrasts the dark, hard, formal, traditional dining space downstairs and the soft, modern bedroom upstairs (opposite).

stencilling on walls, embroidery on furniture, translucent curtains; to the clock on the mantelshelf and the silverware on tables.

Each layer is built on the last. The underlying forms are always simple and direct. They are shaped to be inhabited by real people's touches and glances, responding to real technical requirements for ducts and cupboards, for varied lighting and heating conditions. And then finishing materials, decoration and furnishings are layered, within an underlying, controlling geometry. This is seen in how small spaces are held within the frame of large ones, or in how free-standing furniture elements, however sinuous each may appear alone, cohere to form spaces.

In interior architecture, Mackintosh displays his skill at bringing these varied elements together. Yet this synthesis does not imply sameness, whether between one room and the next, or between the different scales from big building to tiny table.

This is quite a contrast with much of the best work going on around him. The most enduring twentieth-century ideas about architectural design are principles held by Mackintosh's Arts & Crafts contemporaries. To take two examples: first, the inside of a building should be able to be 'read' on its outside; second, the same architectural, formal language which generated overall planning

and silhouette should continue in microcosm into detailed layout, to furnishings and decoration. Frank Lloyd Wright, the last great Arts & Crafts architect and Mackintosh's exact contemporary, was the master of this, and most of the rather few twentieth-century designers who have taken this full range seriously, from building to interior space to door handle, have followed Wright's line. Mackintosh's approach is quite different, as he creates particular (often tiny, sometimes massive) places; layering, overlapping and even contrasting them but not merging and homogenising them. To Mackintosh neither fitment nor decoration is a miniature architecture; each is different in itself, all building together.

Even at The Hill House, on its picturesque and prominent site, the client records that Mackintosh 'submitted his first designs – for the inside only. Not until we had decided on the inside arrangements did he submit drawings of the elevation'. With the second phase of the School of Art, Mackintosh explicitly writes to his client committee: we think it undesirable to commit ourselves to any elevational treatment until the internal arrangement is approved'. This letter from 1908 is far from typical contemporary architectural practice. But we have jumped slightly ahead.

By 1905, Mackintosh might seem at the peak of his career. Yet with what

THE BEDROOM of the Mackintoshes' house, like the dining room, seen opposite, is filled with forms designed before their marriage in 1900 – both rooms have fireplaces brought from their earlier flat. Round the dining table are CRM chairs designed for Argyle Street tea rooms in 1898. Between the bedroom's curvaceous mirror and the bed, above the geometric steel fire surround, is a silvered brass panel made by Margaret Macdonald in 1899.

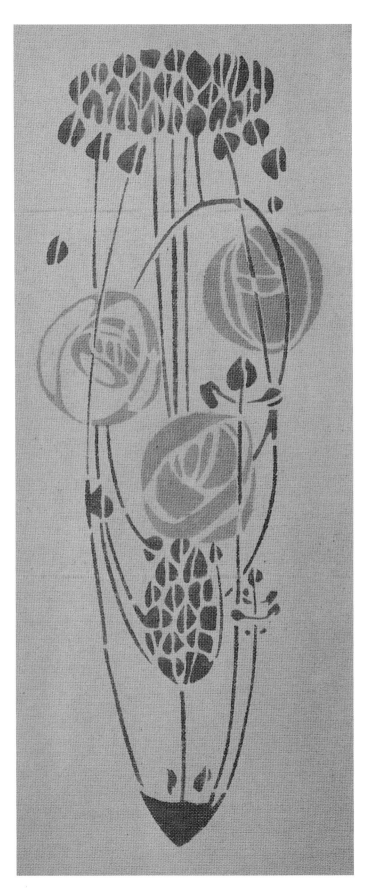

horrifying speed it fades away. There is little new work; with Hous'hill interiors completed and Scotland Street School still slowly building, he only has a dining room for a Berlin exhibition and another interior space for Miss Cranston's in Argyle Street (The Dutch Kitchen, long destroyed). For the first time, Mackintosh takes not his usual one, but two long sketching holidays in England. Is it, though, a loss of direction or nerve as much as of workload? Late in 1905, commissioned for a big country house, he writes to the client that he would design in Tudor or any other English style requested. The result, Achenibert, which takes years to complete, is astonishingly unmemorable, competent Edwardian work; and with no inkling of Margaret's influence. What is up?

At the end of March 1906, Toshie and Margaret, perhaps attempting to recapture the sense of 1900, move from their rented flat to buy an end-of-terrace house in a fashionable middle-class suburb by the University. (Today rebuilt in the Hunterian Art Gallery, University of Glasgow, and open to the public.) The central experience, their L-shaped first-floor room, is unforgettable; a quite unexpected white, spacious calm fills the space. Mackintosh creates a long first-floor window in the south-facing gable wall; the wall between the two rooms is pulled up to stop at the band which runs round the entire area at doorhead. This band (a device Mackintosh learned from the Japanese domestic tradition which fascinated him) frames and encloses the space remarkably, while also extending it horizontally. Where it runs across the tall study window, this band offers translucent pink and purple squares;

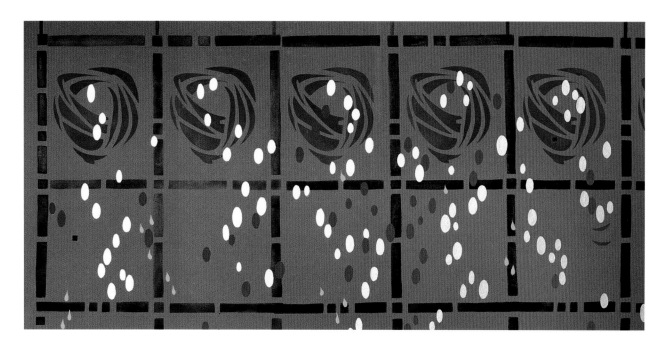

where it runs across the drawing room's typical Victorian bay window, a wall drops down to it, tightening the horizontal geometry of the room.

An impressive space today, the contrast with its neighbouring, cluttered Edwardian interiors would have blown the mind then. Yet it is not extravagant. What is achieved here, with the cheap luxury of cream paint and coloured glass and enamel, is a purity of space and simplicity of form; economy of means, as in the aesthetic dried flower arrangements. Much furnishings and even fitments like fireplaces came with them from their marriage flat. But in a sense they bring more than old bits; as if denying the intervening years, they seem also to bring an earlier sense of the interior. However, here all is Art; perhaps this re-dedication can revitalise his (if not their) creativity?

When Margaret wrote in 1904 to their German friend and influential supporter Hermann Muthesius, that 'the whole town is getting covered with imitations of Mackintosh tea rooms, Mackintosh shops, Mackintosh furniture etc – it is too funny...', it may sound like today. But the contrast is in her next comment, and her distress at all the effort to stamp out the Mackintosh influence. 'I wonder how it will end...' It was an unhappy premonition. Though extraordinarily talented, Mackintosh began as assistant and is now partner in a rather ordinary architectural practice. His work (and its eye to Europe and

HERE IS ONE LITTLE DECORATIVE GEM from each floor of Mackintosh's house (1906): silver snow on a dark rose trellis on the dining room wall, above; a stencilled linen chair-back in the main room, opposite; the light fitting in their bedroom, below.

*THE SECOND PHASE
of the School of Art (1907-9)
develops completely new
surfaces and spaces, yet
within the originally planned
overall form. The library,
opposite, is CRM's spatial
tour de force; complex,
intricate yet intimate. The
narrow gallery which
surrounds the central
clearing runs across the
windows which are seen
from outside, above, as
uncompromising, solid shapes
in glass and masonry.*

even Japan) is now submerged by the current French/American fashion.

His partner Keppie and rival J.J. Burnet had both studied in Paris; Mackintosh is passé, parochial. When he now applies for Fellowship of the Royal Institute of British Architects (RIBA), even that grasping for respectability seems tired and lost.

However, just when they desperately need the work, and even more when Mackintosh needs shaken from depression, at the end of 1906 the School of Art governors are persuaded to complete their building; the original architect, Mackintosh's practice, is commissioned early in 1907. A changed design is inevitable: there are new requirements as well as new fire escape regulations. There is also a new architect in the same skin. The new west half, no longer the work of a precocious but derivative student, is bold, brilliant and entirely personal. And all so cleverly worked that the whole building is a brilliant unity. The new library, behind great oriel windows and unprecedented wall forms, fitting into the same volume as one of the studios (on an 11m square (c.118 sq ft) base), is the most original and complex interior space of his career.

We might expect to see an architect, now aged 41, at the height of his powers, about to produce the work of his maturity. Extraordinarily, Mackintosh will build no more. No other work comes in while the School of Art is under way, beyond a couple more rooms for Miss Cranston in Ingram Street. Two further rooms in the same building follow in 1911, but nothing else over the six years from 1908.

The office has no work (Keppie is equally underemployed) and Mackintosh, depressed, takes to drink; as a colleague recounts, his 'lunch hour often lasts from 1 o'clock to 4.45pm'. When Margaret's sister Frances and her husband Herbert McNair return to Glasgow (sharing the Mackintosh house for a time), neither their marriage nor careers are flourishing. Fra Newbery, also depressive,

CRM DREW FLOWERS all his life, but particularly during his year completely away from architectural work, in Suffolk 1914-15. Japanese Witch Hazel (typically he slightly misspells it on the painting) also has MMM's initials, simply to indicate her presence alongside his.

is ground down by running the Art School – where Keppie, as governor and then chairman, becomes increasingly powerful. By 1912 (and perhaps fearing bankruptcy?) Mackintosh transfers their house into Margaret's name.

In 1913, unable even to complete competition projects which the office is invited to enter, Mackintosh agrees to break with Keppie. But setting up on his own, he still gets no work. He suffers from extreme depression and severe pneumonia. The next June, formalising the end of his partnership, he quickly retreats with Margaret to the Newberys' holiday village in Suffolk for a sketching holiday.

The Last of Glasgow

Perhaps they aim to continue to Vienna; perhaps, refreshed, to try once more in Glasgow. But the European War breaks out and they stay put. For a year, in a complete break from architecture, Mackintosh becomes absorbed in the most elegant and delicate botanical sketches and watercolours (over 40 survive). Then, amidst the xenophobic hysteria drummed up to support the war, traumatically, he is picked up as a spy. His strange Glasgow accent and mysterious appearance in cape and deerstalker, his sketching and long walks in the flat Suffolk landscape at dusk, and indeed letters from Secessionist friends in Vienna, are adequate evidence. Ordered out of East Anglia, the Mackintoshes escape to the more congenial bohemian world of Chelsea, the artist's corner of London, where they live cheaply and happily, though with virtually no work, for eight more years.

In 1916, W.J. Bassett-Lowke, industrialist, model-maker and modernist, looking for an architect, is recommended Mackintosh. Not being found in Glasgow, but eventually tracked to London, Mackintosh agrees to convert Bassett-Lowke's pokey terrace house at 78 Derngate, Northampton. Adding a shallow bay at the back, Mackintosh gives a touch of spaciousness to the bottom floors, frames a balcony to the main bedroom and adds a terrace to the guest room on top. Internally, relocating the stair improves the space. But

what impresses in the interior is the use of bold, deep colour and jagged forms against a shiny black. Here, in the little ground-floor hall, sharp and angry yellow chevrons over black give a jazzy quality (this is rebuilt, and now in Northampton Museum) which is countered in the (later) guest bedroom at the top (rebuilt in the Hunterian Art Gallery, Glasgow), where Mackintosh has dramatic blue/black stripes over wall and ceiling, set off by simple oak furniture. Each of these spaces is powerful and as astonishingly different from the other as from anything he has done before.

From London, Mackintosh designs a basement Cranston tea room, dug out alongside The Willow and, in utter contrast to it, also in shiny blacks and spiky zigzags. These two interiors built in 1917 ('The Dug-Out' and Northampton) show a dark and aggressive sharpness. It is quite different; and it is all the architecture he makes in these years. Both Mackintoshes are designing textiles for various manufacturers (a few hundred designs survive, mostly in the Hunterian), in bright, geometric and sinuous patterns, brilliant and subtle colours. Some derive from art nouveau forms, but are now quite reworked; the generally bold and sharp geometries and colours show the distance they

IN 1916, CRM REMODELS Basset-Lowke's house in Northampton, returning in 1919 to complete designs for the guest bedroom with an abstract geometric decoration in optically violent stripes. (The oak furniture is made to CRM's designs by German prisoners-of-war on the Isle of Man in 1917.) The window-cleaner's view of the room, above, is as reconstructed in the Hunterian Art Gallery.

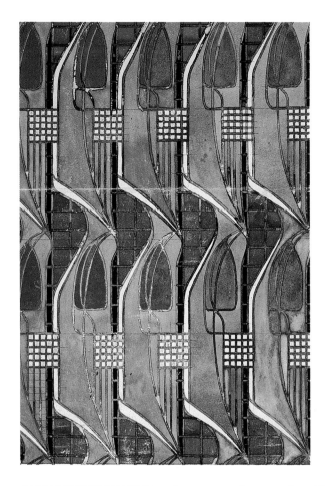

have come from earlier Glasgow work; influences are Vienna and European avant-garde. At the age of 50, Mackintosh's last commission, furniture for Bassett-Lowke, is among his most original, 'modern', and today still his least known.

Margaret and Toshie make a simple life in wartime London as pleasant and congenial as possible. He begins painting studio-based watercolours of flowers and still life. It's when work never recovers with the peace that things get worse. When promised new design commissions fail to materialise, Mackintosh sends pathetic letters – one is for £7 to cover a tax bill – to his friend Davidson, the client of Windyhill now living in the Mackintoshes' own Glasgow house; or begging him to buy a painting for £20 or £30. (Davidson always sends the money.)

In 1920, Bassett-Lowke covers his extraordinary dark hall and stair in light grey; he then asks Mackintosh to design another decorative scheme, and gets a frieze in jazzy triangles and lozenges, but much lighter than before. In 1925 this new frieze is used again in the Bassett-Lowkes' new, larger house. Though the client has tried to commission Mackintosh to design this post-war house itself, this time he could not be tracked down at all.

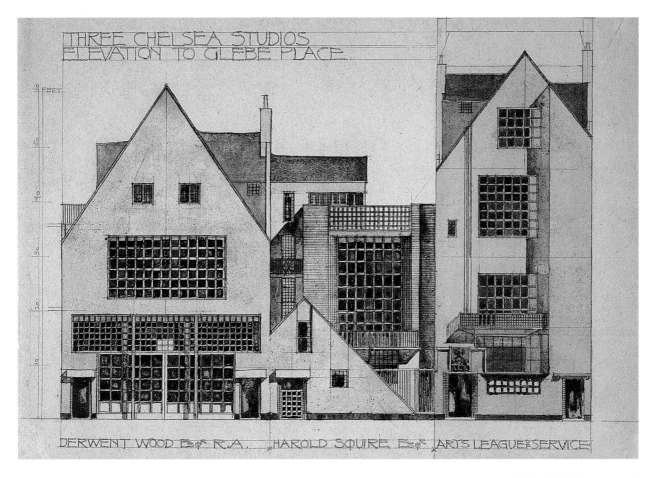

The Artist at 50

After four more unproductive years and in financial difficulty, the Mackintoshes left Britain. Heading for a long Mediterranean holiday, they reach the Roussillon early in 1924. With no incentive to leave, staying in cheap hotels, they finally stop in Port Vendres, on the edge of the mountains by the Franco-Spanish border. Having abandoned architecture for a second and now final time, Mackintosh concentrates again on developing his watercolours. Drained of figures, drained entirely of his earlier symbolism, they move towards a new, almost mute, impersonal vision. The 41 surviving landscapes are ever more architectonic, in their solid patterns and formal relationships of sea, rocks, building shapes, fields. They could hardly be more different from the works of Matisse and those Fauves who painted here a decade earlier. When Margaret takes some to London for exhibition early in 1927, she raises little interest.

Strangely, we now can suddenly see most clearly into this very private couple: when illness forces Margaret back to London, she keeps all Toshie's loving, daily letters to her. These are full of minute observations, of life and gaiety. And work. He records his hard, daily progress on the powerful watercolour *The Rock* through May 1927.

BY 1920, CRM's architectural career seems about to revive, and he spends a busy year working on various building projects in their corner of Chelsea, London. This composite 1920 drawing of three studios gives a hint of what one remarkable group of buildings might have looked like; but nothing gets off the ground. It is a terminal blow. After his last office diary entry in January 1921, virtually no record exists of the Mackintoshes for three years.

'SOON I SHALL START IN OILS,' CRM writes in 1925. But he never does; and, barely affording the watercolours, he describes himself as 'gey sparing wi' the paint'. Three great paintings from 1926-7: the hill town of Fetges, above, which his client at The Hill House buys and gives to The Tate Gallery. The village of Port Vendres features in both Port Vendres, *opposite, and* The Rock, *below. Within very few years, CRM has become a watercolourist of exceptional quality, his compositions increasingly abstract, calm and unpeopled; dominated by geometry, colour and pattern.*

But soon his mouth is so painful that he too is forced back to London, where cancer of the tongue is diagnosed. Early in 1928, following surgery and radium treatment to his mouth, we see him sitting under a tree in the garden of their lodgings in Willow Road, Hampstead; unable to speak. He dies in December 1928, aged 60.

Margaret, never again settled or well, outlives him by just five years. On her death, all their things are valued: his drawings and everything from the studio, all their furniture including several Mackintosh chairs and all the French paintings he was hoping to exhibit. The total valuation is under £90. Later in the year an exhibition is finally got together, in the McLellan Galleries in Glasgow. The friends and former clients who organise it buy much; much more is unrecognised. Most items sell for £15 to £50. One watercolour (a landscape at Port Vendres) is bought by Glasgow Museums.

We look at the wealth of Mackintosh's decorative work, at the great range of objects (over 60 chair designs are documented), at the drawings and masterly paintings, the remarkable interiors carved out within existing shells, and at the very few masterly buildings at the start of the century. Charles Rennie Mackintosh and Frank Lloyd Wright were born within a year of each other. Wright's last major works were built two generations after Mackintosh's career had virtually ended, and 30 years after his death. Fifty years after that death, the professional weekly journal seen by all British architects, *Building Design*, in two polls reported that its readers considered Mackintosh the most important British architect of the last 150 years, the Glasgow School of Art the most important building. It was not always so.

MACKINTOSH, IN HIS 30s, WAS AN EXTRAORDINARY MEMBER of an unremarkable, provincial architectural firm; in the few chances he has to make buildings, he creates a small handful of masterpieces. His name had already been made as artist in graphic decoration, furniture and complete interiors; his hopes are high. Yet by 1910, called old-fashioned, he soon retreats, defeated, giving up architecture for exquisitely observed flower drawings. A huge effort to get back into English architecture yields little beyond glimpses of his fertile imagination. Architecture finally abandoned, he attempts to carve a new niche as watercolourist. His career has been unusual, perhaps too easily seen as tragic; for rather than what might have been, we can marvel at what was achieved.

SELECTED MACKINTOSH WORKS

Glasgow School of Art
167 Renfrew Street,
Glasgow G3 6RQ
Tel: 0141 353 4526
www.gsa.ac.uk

Still a working Art School, the building very much as Mackintosh left it, but with a century of hard use. Also contains important collection of other Mackintosh artefacts. Access by guided tour, Apr-Sept, daily, 10.30am, 11am, 11.30am, 1.30pm, 2pm & 2.30pm. Oct-Mar, Mon-Fri, 11am & 2pm; Sat, 10.30am & 11.30am. The best time to get a fuller view of the building in use is at the annual exhibition of student work in June. Dates and times are worth checking in advance.

Bedroom Fireplace detail, The Hill House, Helensburgh

The Hill House
Upper Colquhoun Drive, Helensburgh G84 9AJ
Tel: 01436 673900   www.nts.org.uk

His domestic masterpiece, now owned by The National Trust for Scotland (NTS). Open daily, Apr-Oct, 1.30-5.30pm, although access is restricted at peak times, and visitors may have to wait until others leave (telephone first).

Helensburgh is 23 miles (37 km) west of Glasgow, and The Hill House is about a mile (1.6 km) up the hill from the station (up Sinclair Street, over the railway by the upper station, then left into Upper Colquhoun Drive). Admission charges apply, NTS and NT members free.

Scotland Street School
225 Scotland Street, Glasgow G5 8QB
Tel: 0141 287 0500   www.glasgowmuseums.com

Closed as a school in 1979. Since 1990, it has become The Museum of Education, open Mon-Thur & Sat, 10am-5pm; Fri & Sun, 11am-5pm; admission free. Period classrooms, exhibitions and other activities. Café.

Windyhill
Kilmacolm

This is a private residence which is not open to the public.

The Mackintosh House
Hunterian Art Gallery
University of Glasgow,
Hillhead Street G12 8QQ
Tel: 0141 330 5431
www.hunterian.gla.ac.uk

Their house reconstructed, alongside a Mackintosh Gallery with changing exhibitions from their Mackintosh collection which also holds 800 of his drawings, paintings and related material. Open Mon-Sat, 9.30am-5pm, gallery but not house closed for lunch. (Reserve collection access available by appointment.) Confirm opening times in advance.

Ingram Street Tea Rooms
For information contact Glasgow Museums,
Tel: 0141 287 2699   www.glasgowmuseums.com

The Kelvingrove Art Galleries has a Glasgow Style gallery which exhibits Ingram Street Tea Room furniture, amidst other work by CRM and his contemporaries. Kelvingrove is due to re-open in 2006 after refurbishment; Ingram Street furniture is on display until late 2005 at the McLellan Galleries, 207 Sauchiehall St, Glasgow G2 3EH; tel 0141 565 4137.

Queen's Cross Church
(Headquarters of the CRM Society)
870 Garscube Road, Glasgow G20 7EL
Tel: 0141 946 6600   Fax: 0141 945 2321
www.crmsociety.com

Mackintosh's only church, this early work is now the headquarters of the Charles Rennie Mackintosh Society and therefore an ideal starting point for a CRM visit. Open Monday to Friday and Sunday afternoons. With the co-operation of all those involved with the Mackintosh heritage, the CRM Society acts as an information centre, and it is able to arrange guided tours to suit most requirements.

The House for an Art Lover
Bellahouston Park, Dumbreck Road, Glasgow.
Tel: 0141 353 4770   www.houseforanartlover.co.uk

Exhibition/café/design shop open daily, 10am-5pm. Admission charges apply.